Small Talk:

How to Connect Effortlessly with Anyone!

Strike up conversations with confidence and make small talk without the fear of being awkward

Written by Betty Bohm

Download The Audiobook FREE!

Read this first

I want to show my appreciation for supporting my work so I would like to give you <u>this audiobook version</u> 100% FREE!. (alternatively, go here: www.smalltalkskills.com/freeaudiobook)

Copyright: Published in the United States by Jandalman Publishing

All rights Reserved. No part of this publication or the information in it may be quoted from or reproduced in any form by means such as printing, scanning, photocopying or otherwise without prior written permission of the copyright holder.

Disclaimer and Terms of Use: Effort has been made to ensure that the information in this book is accurate and complete, however, the author and the publisher do not warrant the accuracy of the information, text and graphics contained within the book due to the rapidly changing nature of science, research, known and unknown facts and internet. The Author and the publisher do not hold any responsibility for errors, omissions or contrary interpretation of the subject matter herein. This book is presented solely for motivational and informational purposes only.

Modified Dog Image from Flickr user <u>torbakhopper</u> (https://www.flickr.com/photos/gazeronly/7282874924/)

Thank you for your support of the Author's rights.

www.jandalmanpublishing.com

For orders, please email:

dave@jandalmanpublishing.com

Table of Contents

Introduction 1

Chapter 1: Exploring Your Assumptions About Small Talk 3

Chapter 2: Common Challenges People Have With Small Talk 15

Chapter 3: Feeling Stuck For Small Talk Words? 19

Chapter 4: Small Talk Has Its Benefits 28

Chapter 5: See How Successful Small Talk Works In Practice 32

Chapter 6: Enhance Your Credibility In Small Talk Situations 59

Chapter 7: Social Cues To Give You Small Talk Clues 78

Chapter 8: Tips On Getting The Most From Your Small Talk Encounters ... 87

Final Words 102

Appendix 103

Glossary 106

Urgent Plea! 108

Introduction

This guide attempts to help you gain a better insight into your own understanding and views about small talk and the purpose it may serve, for you, and for others. It has been written to get you thinking about how you may wish to interact with others in small talk, how you can become comfortable doing this and still maintain your own voice.

If you already are a confident small talker then some of the other strategies in this guide will help you to enhance what you've already got. If you are the kind of person who fears talking with strangers or avoids small talk for other reasons then this book could help you to examine your assumptions regarding small talk, examine what it means to take a risk and encourage your personal reflections on small talking stereotypes. Throughout the guide there are examples of small talk dialogue and suggestions on how to approach small talk situations.

This book is not going to turn you into a small-talking robot! Far from it. What it will give you is your unique collection of your own practical examples about how to develop your small talk topics, how to individualize your own approaches when engaging in small talk, and strategies to help you feel more comfortable during small talk encounters.

You can follow the wide range of guided questions for reflection, so that you can develop your 'small talk skills' in an easy-to-follow, step-by-step way. These questions are designed to ensure that you get the most out of your small talk interactions with strangers and acquaintances. With practice ideas offered to you in the book, you will be learning how to shape your small talk conversations and experiences, understanding how to individualize your approaches, and creating a personal portfolio of patterns used in small talk that will help you converse more fluently and naturally.

Engaging in small talk with confidence is the key and using the appropriate language can make a huge difference in the outcome of any situation. This guide touches on gender differences and how they play out, not only in our fears, but also the outcome of an interaction. Your ability to pick up on key social cues will help you handle different situations in different ways. Additionally, the guide explores the reasons and benefits of small talk for you and others.

This small talk guide examines the technical aspects of small talk, such as, where small talk comes from, the various purposes it serves and how it works. There are simple explanations regarding social cues and tips on how to remove yourself from uncomfortable small talk situations.

Finally, the book offers ideas on getting the most from the small talk experiences you have every day. There are practical strategies to try at home and in social settings and you'll learn to navigate the ups and downs of conversations.

Chapter 1: Exploring Your Assumptions About Small Talk

I don't have the time for small talk!

With the many demands on our time these days, some people might say that they simply don't have time for small talk anymore. Commuting to work, rushing from one meeting to another, picking kids up and dropping them off, getting groceries, taking some exercise, looking after family and friends, it's a never-ending list of regular activities for us to do. However, the case may well be that all of these activities offer us opportunities to engage in small talk, if, and here's the big '*if*' we decide to view it that way.

Much of your outlook about taking the time to engage in small talk will depend on how you measure your time, and how you like to spend your time. How do you like to spend your time? Chatting with friends, family and colleagues? Or do you prefer to do activities where you give your mouth and ears a rest? Like meditation? or jogging? or relaxing reading? or creative painting? Whatever you like to do with your spare time depends very much on your own personal preferences and situations which are unique to you.

Let's deal with measuring time first. Of course, it's really very easy to measure time. All you have to do is look at your watch or a clock, mark the start time, and then when an activity is finished, mark the stop time. Now we do this for most of our daily activities whether we are measuring time precisely or measuring it approximately.

Have you ever tried measuring your small talk time? Whichever way you choose to measure it, it should prove to be very illuminating for you and provide you with some insights into how much or how little small talk you actually engage in.

The common theme that runs through the amount of time we spend doing the things we like to do springs from our ability to focus so that we can live fully in that very moment - whatever it is! And the same goes for our interactions with each other in small talk.

This book is going to help you get a sense of what you actually think about small talk and what may be holding you back from doing it.

Small talk is only for time wasters, brown nosers, fuddy-duddies and busy bodies, isn't it?

There can be quite a lot of negativity around small talk. This might be because there are so many different views on what it is and what it isn't.

Some people think it's a waste of time. Why converse about unimportant things when you could be talking about more significant or more meaningful topics that interest you? Others might see small talk as a way to ingratiate themselves with people they want to be liked by or they see as being useful to them. Many younger generations might say that small talk is for 'old' fuddy-duddies, who are over-polite with one another, and only 'do' small talk out of a sense of tradition. For many, small talk might seem like a nosy parker's way of finding out more about you and your business. These are just a few of the ways of looking at small talk of course, there are many more.

According to the Cambridge online dictionary, small talk is *'conversation about things that are not important, often between people who do not know each other well'.*

When you read this, you have to think to yourself, 'Why do we even bother with small talk'? If it is only to converse about unimportant things with strangers or acquaintances, then why do we do it? If you look at small talk in this way, then it probably won't hold much attraction for you. However, there must be something in small talk that goes beyond the superficiality because people around the world engage in small talk every day.

Thinking about your own views:

- What sort of strategies do you use to engage people in small talk?
- What sort of responses do you typically get from people?

Take a small talk risk

Engaging someone in small talk can definitely feel like taking a bit of a risk! And it can be tricky to get off to the right start in small talk. Plus it's hard to know where small talk begins and where it ends. This can make people feel unsure about it, and when we feel unsure about something then we are less likely to want to do it. The major difference between chit-chat and small talk is that small talk is typically carried out between strangers, whereas chit-chat is not necessarily between strangers – you can chit-chat with friends and family. This may be another clue about the reasons why people might find small talk uncomfortable - it involves people we don't know or don't know well, so there is more cause for embarrassment if the small talk doesn't work out.

Here are a few tips to help you feel more confident when small talking. A few basic principles to do with politeness can help you get off to a good start. Professor Lakoff, who is a well-known expert in linguistics, explained that there are three main principles of politeness:

1. Be friendly
2. Don't impose
3. Give options

It would be nice to think that we all have a firm grasp of how to use these principles in practice, but in reality we don't all interpret or demonstrate politeness in the same way. If you make a point to stay alert to them and build up a better awareness of how these principles work, it should help you to successfully engage in small talk. You can do this by keeping tabs on various small talk scenarios that happen around you even if you're not directly involved in them! Try to keep your eyes and ears open by watching people's polite interactions.

To help you do this, let's look at each principle in a little more detail.

- **Being Friendly**: Making the first move in small talk often requires a friendly approach. It also requires a reciprocated friendly approach in order for it to work well.

- **Not Imposing**: we shouldn't try to force someone to accept something they don't want, or a belief that we may hold true for ourselves but is not necessarily shared by others. Small talk can have a superficial nature, so it is very unlikely that a person will try to impose their beliefs onto you during small talk. If a person does try to impose something on you and it makes you feel uncomfortable, then it's likely that the person doesn't know how to engage in successful small talk, and therefore, it is acceptable for you to end the small talk encounter, and if necessary to remove yourself from the situation.

- **Giving Options**: one simple way to try to understand giving and receiving options in small talk is to think about ways in which you could either opt in or opt out of small talk. Whenever we are engaged in small talk we should be alert to the idea of giving people options (including ourselves) as well as responding to options offered by other people.

Here is quite a typical social scenario where you can offer options. Imagine you are in a rush to get somewhere, and a researcher conducting a survey in some public place wishes to engage with you in small talk with the view to asking you to take part in the survey. It may well be the case that you want to take part in the survey, but on this occasion, you simply don't have the time. You might decide to signal to the researcher that you have opted out for this in the present moment, but that you might opt in later.

The small talk scenario could play out like this:

Passerby: **"Sorry, I'm actually running late and I'm in a rush, but when I'm on my way back I might have time then, okay?"**

Researcher: **"Yes, sure."**

In this small talk scenario, the passerby gave himself options to opt in or to opt out of doing the survey. Similarly, the passerby gave the researcher an option to interview him later.

Here is another common day small talk situation with options:

Passerby: **"I can't help but notice that you look a little lost."**

Stranger: **"Actually yes, I'm looking for the post office. Do you know where it is?"**

OR

Stranger: **"I'm fine, but thank you."**

Providing people with options to opt in or opt out - no matter whether they are strangers or acquaintances can help to minimize embarrassing or awkward moments during small talk encounters.

Being comfortable with 'doing' small talk

Have you ever heard someone saying: "I don't enjoy parties where I have to make small talk with complete strangers"? Small talk can be a real turn-off for some people because it can seem pretty false, requires people to make a bit of an effort and can be awkward particularly when small talking with strangers. On the other hand, when you are small talking with someone, it can sometimes help you feel more at ease, and when a person is showing polite behavior toward you this can make you feel good. Unfortunately, politeness is not highly rated by everyone! Impoliteness is typically seen as negative behavior and by choosing to not engage in small talk you may be perceived by others as impolite, or worse, anti-social. You may genuinely feel unable to engage with people in small talk. However, think about it like this: if you view politeness as quite a positive behavior in yourself and in others, then you may be more likely to view small talk as beneficial to you, and maybe you'd be more willing to give small talk a go!

Here are two questions for you:

1. How do you respond to other people's politeness?

2. Do you see politeness as an important aspect of your interactions with others?

Depending on your personal answers to these questions, the benefits or drawbacks of politeness in society may also have some influence of how you view the role of small talk in your life. This is something you need to think about and try to understand because your personal views on politeness may be influencing your desire to engage in small talk. Experts in small talk use various aspects of politeness to ensure the recipient feels comfortable. They do this because they are keenly aware that the politeness concept is fundamental to successful small talk.

Some people may be confident conversationalists or good at holding discussions but less good at small talk or chit chat. Why is this? Some people might say that small talk or chit chat relies on being interested in others, and being willing to converse with a wide range of people. Other people might say that being able to hold a discussion is much more difficult than doing small talk and that it serves a different purpose, for instance, in business meetings, debates and negotiations. However, small talk can help ease pressurized conversations and discussions because you are showing your politeness to others. People find it hard to ignore genuine politeness in others. Politeness can be a useful small talk tool for you in any situation you may find yourself.

Small talk avoidance - why and when does this happen?

Here are three questions for you:

1. Do you think you actively try to avoid small talk?
2. Do you avoid small talk in certain social situations or with certain people?
3. What sort of strategies do you use to avoid small talk encounters?

Some people have problems with engaging with small talk, not because they are unfriendly and impolite individuals but because they don't want to draw attention to themselves in unfamiliar social settings. This is particularly when they are likely to meet people they don't know or don't know very well and this is understandable. Engaging in small talk with work colleagues or business acquaintances can be really complicated and challenging for some. Sometimes small talk leads to other forms of social communication, such as a discussion, and it's often hard to know where the small talk ends. All of these reasons can make people feel unsure about engaging in small talk, and this may result in trying to avoid social situations where small talk is likely to occur.

Cautionary advice on small talk stereotypes

A lot of books and websites offer advice on small talk. They comment about personality traits, such as, extroverts and introverts. A stereotypical view is that extroverts find it easier to engage in small talk because they tend to be talkative and outgoing. Likewise, if you believe in stereotyping, then it is trickier for introverts to engage in small talk because they tend to be shy and less communicative in social situations. However, dividing the entire population into only two personality traits doesn't give us the whole picture because there are more ways to describe a human's personality. According to leading researchers in personality psychology, there are five main personality traits that can be used to describe a human's personality.

These personality traits are divided into five domains:

- Openness to experience
- Conscientiousness
- Extraversion
- Agreeableness
- Neuroticism

As you can see, extroversion is only one of the personality traits. The level of extroversion and sociability can be portrayed on a sliding scale with very outgoing on one end and solitary on the other end. An often-overlooked aspect of extroversion is the level of surgency in a person. Surgency includes a person's reactivity to emotions and to their environment. It is also connected to a person's ability to be fluent in both speech and writing. It could be that people who feel that they are fluent in speech and writing are more likely to engage in small talk, not necessarily because they are more outgoing than anybody else, but because they feel able to communicate with fluency. If you don't feel you can speak easily, or well, and if you worry about being understood you may not feel like engaging in small talk.

Here are three questions for you:

1. How would you rate your level of fluency in your native language?

2. Do you feel you are more confident in writing or in speech?

3. Do you tend to feel energized or drained by social surroundings?

The last question is an important one because it asks you about your emotional reactivity to your surroundings. It is important for another reason too. It is linked to context - the situation in which something exists or happens. It is worth bearing in mind that your level of engagement in small talk is not necessarily dependent on your personality trait, the context in which the small talk takes place can be very important too.

I've put together a special resources pack that I'll be adding to over time. These resources compliment the book. Download the action pack now and put some of the points raised here into action. The key to making changes in the way you talk with others is to apply small and measureable experiments and reflect on how they go. This resource pack will help you on your way to feeling comfortable in any social situation. Just click the link below:

<u>Take action and get the free resources pack now!</u>

Type this into your browser

http://smalltalkskills.com/book-resources

Chapter 2: Common Challenges People Have With Small Talk

Who do you really need to engage in small talk?

Imagine a scenario which you might observe in a public place, where a couple are waiting to be served at a restaurant, or are waiting for a take-away pizza.

Here is a question for you:

Are they likely to be *small* talking to each other?

You could say that the reason why they aren't small talking to each other is because they've had a bust-up row and are cooling off. But have you considered it from another perspective? Quite a lot of the time couples simply don't feel the need to engage in small talk with each other. Perhaps it is because they are intimate with one another, and therefore, they don't feel the need to engage in small talk. In other words, the social relationships we have, and the level of intimacy we consider we have in these relationships influence who we engage in small talk with and who we don't.

It's possible that the more we know someone, the less likely we feel the need to small talk with them. And the reverse could be true. The less we know someone, the more we need to small talk with them. This point is worth remembering when contemplating who you should engage in small talk with and the possible reasons for you to do so.

Considering your relationships between business acquaintances and work colleagues, it could be said that because we don't share a high level of social intimacy with them, it means we are more likely to feel the need to engage in some aspects of small talk while at work or when travelling on business together. Some people feel the need to engage in small talk, as a way to present and support a positive self-image as being cooperative, and desirous of a harmonious and productive workplace or business relationship. Also, some people wish to influence what other people think of their position of power and status by engaging in small talk in certain ways. When we look at things from this perspective, small talk can become quite a complex scenario and quite a challenging experience.

'On the go' technologies and small talk

Love them or hate them - mobile or cell phones and hand-held devices, such as, phones, iPads and laptops are very much part of our everyday lives. As you will no doubt be aware, some people interact with use them more than others. In this world of digital mobile devices, it seems to be getting harder and harder to know when it is acceptable to engage in small talk and when it isn't. It is not clear yet whether there are long-term benefits or drawbacks to being fully engrossed in digital mobile devices on a regular basis. What can be said is that the world looks and sounds very different to the pre-digital and pre-mobile phone technology era.

If we never look up from our mobile phones or laptops the entire time we are taking a journey on public transport or waiting in a queue, does it mean we want to close ourselves off from others who happen to be around us? Does it mean that we don't enjoy social interactions with strangers, acquaintances or even our friends anymore? The answers to these questions will depend on you and how you like to interact with other people around you.

Does small talk stand a chance in today's world? It depends which way you look at it. Some might say that when a room full of people are looking down and only two people are looking up; it's easier to identify people with whom you can make small talk. This is quite a positive way of looking at things. On the other hand, if a room full of people are only looking down because they don't have anyone to engage with in small talk, then that's quite a negative outlook, don't you think?

The main point here is that everyone is different. Some people definitely go out of their way to engage people in small talk while others do everything in their power to avoid it. The way you view small talk will no doubt be based on your own past experiences of engaging in small talk and whether you found them an enjoyable or an annoying aspect of everyday life.

Should you small talk with people you don't like?

It's a fact of life that people don't like everyone they meet. Should you engage in small talk with people you don't like? Some people would say 'no' outright by reasoning that it is insincere to engage in small talk with people they don't like. This reaction is understandable. Quite a lot of your decision making about who you wish to talk to, or not to talk to, is based on how you feel about a person or group of people. The question of whether you consider a person to be trustworthy or not also comes into play and can influence your decision about whether you like someone or not and whether you can believe that person or not. There may be sound reasons for avoiding specific people who you have decided you don't like or you don't trust and the decisions you make are likely to be complex, challenging and dynamic. Let's look at things a different way: have you ever found yourself changing your mind about a person whereby a person who you thought you liked, you find you don't? Or a person who you thought you didn't like, you changed your mind about, and now you like that person?

We can accept that it is easier to engage with people we know or think we like in small talk, so why go to the effort of talking to people we don't like? There are two reasons to try to be open-minded about engaging with a person or group of people you don't like. First, you really need to be sure that you know you don't like the person. This is different from the situation when you think you don't like someone. This is even more crucial to bear in mind when you are trying to establish whether someone likes you or not. Have you ever had an experience whereby you thought that a person didn't like you because they never engaged in small talk with you and then eventually over time you find out that they are actually painfully shy even though you originally thought they were being standoffish with you? Second, you need to decide if engaging in successful small talk with everybody is useful or beneficial to you. Some of your decisions about this may be based on the sort of activities you are involved in and the people with whom you come into contact. Business people, entrepreneurs, community leaders, managers and psychologists are often quoted saying that small talk can make a difference in people's lives, careers, work and community involvement. Therefore, it is worth taking the time to decide whether small talk can be valuable to you.

Chapter 3: Feeling Stuck For Small Talk Words?

How do you know what to talk about in small talk situations?

One commonly cited assumption is that men like to engage in small talk topics that cover sports, current affairs and politics, while women like to engage in topics about family, relationships and hobbies. There are many more bits of advice like this on the Web. Have you considered that the people who offer this advice are not aware of their own assumptions, and so they pass on their assumptions to others as 'advice', even when these assumptions aren't necessarily your own? Another commonly held assumption shared by many is that women speak more than men, and if this is true, then men must speak less than women. This means that if women speak more than men, then men must be listening more than women. However, another popular assumption is that men are more comfortable talking about themselves than women are. With so many different points-of-view about this - it's hard to know what to think for yourself!

The hallmark of successful small talk is when people take turns to speak and to listen. Turn-taking is a social communication skill because it involves taking turns to speak and to listen. This means that when someone speaks, the other person is typically meant to be listening. The reverse is true: when someone listens, the other person is typically meant to be speaking. Turn-taking is a powerful attribute of small talk. The functions used in small talk are also powerful because they influence the way the small talk plays out. Let's look at a small talk scenario that could occur between a man and a woman.

For all dialogue sections a full reading of the dialogue will be presented. Then a section of the same dialogue will follow and outline the various functions associated with each dialogue reading.

Man: **"Clara's English has come along leaps and bounds lately."**

Woman: **"She's gotten really good, hasn't she?"**

Man: **"She's so good I'd never have known English wasn't her mother tongue. In fact, she corrected my English last week!"**

Woman: {little laugh} **"She is also fluent in Spanish and Italian."**

Man: **"She certainly has a way with words!"**

Below is the previous dialogue explained line-by-line.

Man: **"Clara's English has come along leaps and bounds lately."**

[this shows how to make a compliment about somebody]

Woman: **"She's gotten really good, hasn't she?"**

[this shows agreement with a question seeking your agreement]

Man: **"She's so good I'd never have known English wasn't her mother tongue. In fact, she corrected my English last week!"**

[this shows an enthusiastic agreement with a self-deprecating comment]

Woman: {little laugh} **"She is also fluent in Spanish and Italian."**

[this offers new or supplementary information]

Man: "**She certainly has a way with words!**"

[this shows how to enthusiastically affirm understanding of information]

This scenario displays successful small talk - both people took their turns to listen and to speak, both responded appropriately to the functions [*compliment someone, agree, ask a question seeking further agreement*] and neither person spoke or listened more than the other person. It is important to remember the power of turn-taking when engaging in small talk, as it is more likely to influence your small talk experiences than gender differences. In most small talk scenarios, the set pattern of turn-taking means that people are looking and waiting for their social cues, like for example, when a man offers for a woman to pass first through a doorway, and the woman acknowledges this by smiling or saying 'thank you'.

In small talk, the speed of turn-taking can also appear to go faster than in long conversations and discussions. The speed of turn-taking can make people feel under pressure because they know they haven't got long before it is their turn to say something. This does take a bit of getting used to, and the more you can anticipate the set pattern of turn-taking, the more comfortable you will feel with the speed. Of course, it is not a race to say something quickly, but it is a feature of small talk that is worth paying attention to.

Is small talk easier with the same sex or the opposite sex?

This sounds like a strange question doesn't it? And it most probably is. Why? It could be because you've never really stopped to give it much thought before, so it could be unfamiliar territory for you. It could also be that small talk is hard enough to do well without having to think about differences in speaking and listening styles between men and women. In recent decades, there has been a lot of research into communication styles between genders which means that it is puzzling to make sense of it at all. My advice is to decide for yourself. Let's look at how you might arrive at your own decisions. It is quite useful to spend some time thinking about how you currently approach the opposite sex in small talk:

Here are four questions for you:

Answer these questions when considering a conversation with, firstly, the same sex and, secondly, the opposite sex.

1. Do you select different topics?
2. Do you find you are speaking more or do you find you are listening more?
3. Do you find you are more hesitant in your turn-taking?
4. Do you feel more at a loss of what to say next in your turn-taking patterns?

There's nothing wrong if you have answered 'yes' to any of these questions. If you have, it suggests that you acknowledge some of the subtle differences that you might be experiencing when engaging the opposite sex in small talk. You may simply feel more comfortable engaging in small talk with someone of the same sex as you, and therefore, any subtle differences that you experience when talking to the opposite sex might seem a little strange or uncomfortable. This is understandable. Naturally, there is no right or wrong way to engage the opposite sex in small talk. The best thing you can do is to be aware of any assumptions that you might hold about what the opposite sex likes or doesn't like. There isn't one best way to do this, but there will be a way that feels right for you.

Try to think about these questions next time you're small talking with someone from the opposite sex:

Here are two questions for you:

1. What do you find you notice about yourself?

2. Are you making a conscious effort to direct the small talk in a certain way?

The best advice I can offer here is that being yourself is going to help you feel more comfortable and confident in the long-run. You may think it helps to change yourself to fit in with a stereotyped version of small talk with the opposite sex, but have you thought of it this way: the differences between men and women are what make us feel most interested in each other because we have more opportunity to learn about our differences? Small talk with the same sex might mean that we take the similarities for granted. It's worth thinking about.

What makes people feel hesitant or feel tongue-tied?

It is important to try to understand whether or not your perspective of what makes you feel comfortable or uncomfortable in small talk is actually influenced by the opposite sex or by the context which influences how you feel. The small talk context in which you engage, or choose not to engage in, is paramount to your understanding and perception of what is, and what is not going on in a social situation.

This is why using your social cues is extremely important to you.

Your ability to respond to social cues may be dependent on two things:

1. your level of oxytocin (also known at the 'social hormone' or the 'bonding hormone')
2. whether you have social cue impairments (such as social anxiety)

The level of oxytocin is a really interesting physiological phenomenon which occurs in humans and research evidence suggests that this hormone helps us to decide who we want to trust and who we wish to bond with. It could be that this hormone helps us make decisions about who we are most likely to accept or reject in social situations. While more needs to be discovered about this hormone and how it affects our ability to perceive social cues, there is some indication that it plays an important role in helping us use our social radar.

It's common for us to feel hesitant in small talk situations, particularly when we are unfamiliar with the place, and the people who inhabit our new surroundings. It is also quite likely that we feel hesitant around people with whom we don't feel a social connection, and perhaps this is because we have used our social radar, rightly or wrongly, to work out whether we want to socially bond with this person, or not. Therefore, hesitancy or a loss of words may have little to do with a person's gender, it may have more to do with how our social radar, oxytocin hormone and perception of social cues combine together to help us feel comfortable and secure with the people in our surroundings.

Here are two questions for you:

1. Have you ever felt a strong bond with someone even though you don't know them well?

2. Have you ever thought you don't like someone even though they are a complete stranger?

Our social radar possibly has something to do with the way we respond to individuals or groups of people. Mostly, the social radar will tell us if we identify with people or not, meaning are we similar to others in some way? We are more likely to engage in small talk with people who we think are similar to us than with those where we perceive differences. This is understandable. Some of our decision making about engaging with others who look and sound different will also be influenced by personality traits, such as level of openness to new experiences and agreeableness.

I've put together a special resources pack that I'll be adding to over time. These resources compliment the book. Download the action pack now and put some of the points raised here into action. The key to making changes in the way you talk with others is to apply small and measureable experiments and reflect on how they go. This resource pack will help you on your way to feeling comfortable in any social situation. Just click the link below:

<u>Take action and get the free resources pack now!</u>

Type this into your browser

http://smalltalkskills.com/book-resources

Chapter 4: Small Talk Has Its Benefits

What is the point of small talk?

This may seem like a daft question. However, it is important to try to answer this question because it helps us to understand some of the possible social purposes of small talk. On the face of things, it might seem that small talk isn't actually *'for'* anything in particular. In other words, there doesn't appear to be any strong argument to convince a person to engage in small talk or not to engage in small talk.

Two British comedians (Alexander Armstrong and Ben Miller) portray the origin of small talk in one of their comedy sketches.

To view the video of the sketch type this link into your browser: www.smalltalkskills.com/history

In the sketch, two cavemen are waiting for mammoth to appear. There is a silence between them. One caveman breaks the silence by saying: "Me like mammoth." The other caveman agrees that he likes mammoth too. And funnily enough, small talk has begun! The point of small talk between the two cavemen in this scenario is that of a space filler or as a way to pass the time. This is quite likely how small talk came into existence, as a socially communicative way of passing time in each other's company or filling silences.

However, this may not be the only reason to engage in small talk. If we look again at the comedy sketch, we can observe that there is something else going on between the two cavemen. The two cavemen agree that both of them have something in common - they both like mammoth. One caveman asks: "What you do?" The other replies: "Hunter gatherer." This exchange of information is quite useful to the cavemen. Firstly, they have established that they have a common goal; to hunt the mammoth. This information may prove useful particularly if they want to help each other to hunt and kill the mammoth. This exchange of social communication signals cooperative behavior. When people show they might be willing to cooperate with each other in a social situation, they are portraying their friendly intentions, and quite possibly, that they desire some sort of positive and cooperative interaction with each other.

Why small talk might be good for you

Some people get quite a buzz from engaging in small talk. It can feel quite pleasurable and even special. Why is this sometimes the case? When we look at the various elements of small talk, it may be easier to see why small talk can help you feel energized. Let's look at why this may be.

If someone is polite to you, then they are demonstrating some social aspects. Not only are they revealing something about themselves but also how they regard you - they are showing you that they care about your feelings. This is most important to remember. Most people would agree that they would prefer someone to be polite, friendly and cooperative toward them rather than be impolite, unfriendly and uncooperative. Perhaps this is why small talk can be powerful in some contexts especially when you are in an unfamiliar environment or when there are a lot of strangers around you. You need to feel that people are going to cooperate with you - help you if you have a question or need something.

Cooperative behavior in small talk helps us feel more secure, probably because there is a commonly-held perception that the more you cooperate with someone, the more likely they will cooperate with you. This doesn't always turn out to be the case, but experts in small talk are aware of the possible benefits of displaying cooperative behavior; not only for themselves, but also for other people involved in small talk and even for the people who might be observing small talk, like for example, other people sitting on a bus.

In a world that seems constantly awash with people on 'send' mode, as in send an email, send a text, post a comment on a blog, write a book and even present a topic on YouTube, it is quite hard to know if anyone is actually listening to you. It's also quite hard to know if anyone actually *wants* to listen to you! Notice the emphasis on listening in small talk. Listening to the other person is a really crucial aspect to successful small talk and could be a good reason why people get a little kick out of engaging in small talk. People feel more valued especially when they can see and hear that someone is listening to them.

There is possibly another benefit to small talk. While small talk can be quite mindless, (How are you? Fine thanks and you? Fine thanks) - it isn't always mindless! In some respects, engaging in small talk can actually help you to discover new information particularly about a place you are unfamiliar with or about people with whom you are not yet acquainted. In this sense, engaging in small talk could be good for you because it could bring you new information or new insights that you might never have received had it not been for a friendly small talk encounter.

Why small talk might be good for other people

The various elements of small talk (politeness, turn-taking and social cues), when combined appropriately, can make for a more powerful and more persuasive reason for people to engage in small talk, and the same probably holds true for the benefits of small talk for other people.

It could be that the stranger on the bus has been through some difficulties in life and the chance to engage in small talk takes on a bigger meaning for that person than it does for you. This is a fundamental difference. You may be completely unaware of the possible small talk benefits for other people. This is especially important to bear in mind if you don't know the person. We all have it within us to smile at someone, and most of the time this will lift our mood, and the mood of others too. It's a big shame when people are so wrapped up in their own life bubbles that they remain oblivious to what is going on around them. We can, and should remember to be more available to others even if it is just a quick "hi how are you?" especially when you are out doing your daily activities because in reality most people are trying to go about their everyday chores and the similarities between us are probably greater than we think. So, in that respect, making a small talk comment about shopping, getting the car fixed, picking up the dry cleaning, or buying paint to redecorate - are all ways that we can enrich our lives even when involved in mundane activities.

Chapter 5: See How Successful Small Talk Works In Practice

How does small talk work?

Children typically learn how to hold a conversation from watching their parents having a conversation. Also, our parents may have helped us to participate in our own conversations by helping us to understand how to take turns in a conversation.

Picture this familiar scenario on a public bus. A parent and child are on the bus. The child drops a toy. A stranger sitting nearby picks up the child's toy and hands it back to the child and says: "Here you go." The child takes the toy and says nothing.

Parent says to child: **"And what do you say?"**

The child hesitates.

The parent continues: **"Say, thank you."**

Child: **"Thank you."**

The parent had probably intended to teach the child a number of things from this seemingly superficial experience involving small talk. Firstly, the parent wants to teach the child how to show the stranger that being polite shows people that you care about their feelings.

Picture how the scenario might continue.

The stranger smiles and says: **"How old is your kid?"**

Parent smiles, and says to child: **"Go on, tell us how old you are!"**

The child looks at parent and then says to stranger. **"Three."**

Secondly, the parent wants to teach the child about how to take turns in a social situation, particularly with strangers. Turn-taking also seems like a reasonable skill to teach a child because it enables the child to build meaning around the context of the social situation. For instance, a child learns how to build meaning in a conversation by answering a question. When you look back at the overall experience, the child is learning how to demonstrate desirable behavior in society (politeness) and how to demonstrate turn-taking. Turn-taking is a useful communication skill that helps people build meaning around language and context.

Another vital aspect of small talk is how to read a person's social cues. The child took language cues from the parent about what the child should say in each part of the small talk conversation. The experience also teaches the child about how to demonstrate a certain kind of human behavior which is seen as desirable in society. The behavior demonstrated in this scenario is summed up in the saying, 'one good turn deserves another' - because the stranger picked up the toy and returned it to the child, the child is cued to say something in return for this friendly and considerate action. The child has not only picked up on the parent's language cues, but has also picked up on the stranger's behavioral cues.

To say that small talk only requires people to demonstrate politeness and to take their social cues would simplify things. But from a child's point of view:

Politeness and turn-taking and social cues equals the basics

about how to socially interact in small talk.

Seeing the set patterns and getting the functions right

There is no denying it, small talk happens all around and it probably happens quite a few times during the day or the week depending on where you go and what you are doing. Brief interludes of small talk that you see, hear or engage in form a physical context and also a social context around your daily activities.

The type of small talk that occurs in your surroundings is often context specific. In other words, different social contexts demand different types of small talk; some small talk contexts require you to follow a set pattern of turn-taking whereas other contexts can allow for a wider variety of turn-taking.

Here are a couple of examples of set patterns of turn-taking. This is easier to understand if you think about actors reading from a script, such as a screenplay, radio play or theatre play.

The theatre actors are playing characters from a bygone era. They are rehearsing their lines from a script. The italicized words in brackets illustrate the function of the language being used in small talk.

This next example revolves around offering a person some new information and expressing levels of certainty and uncertainty about the new information.

Actor 1: **"Beautiful weather we're having, wouldn't you say?"**

Actor 2: **"Yes, rather. Not sure how long it's going to last though."**

Actor 1: **"Until Wednesday they say."**

Actor 2: **"I see. Well, one can never be too sure."**

Actor 1: **"Right, well then, must dash to get this letter off."**

Actor 2: **"Ah yes, of course."**

Below is the previous dialogue explained line-by-line.

Actor 1: **"Beautiful weather we're having, wouldn't you say?"**

[this is a statement about surroundings and a question seeking your agreement]

Actor 2: **"Yes, rather. Not sure how long it's going to last though."**

[this is an agreement and a statement of uncertainty about something]

Actor 1: **"Until Wednesday they say."**

[this shows new information to make something more certain]

Actor 2: **"I see. Well, one can never be too sure."**

[this affirms understanding of information and offers new information of uncertainty]

Actor 1: **"Right, well then, must dash to get this letter off."**

[this signals the ending of small talk]

Actor 2: **"Yes, of course."**

[this acknowledges the ending]

This is useful because it reveals some of the set patterns that are involved in small talk.

This next example revolves around complimenting a person and expressing levels of agreement about the compliment and some additional information to support the credibility of the person's compliment.

Actor 2: **"I say, Marianne is a bit of a whizz at tennis!"**

Actor 1: **"She is rather good, isn't she?"**

Actor 2: **"She's more than good - she's beaten me three times this week!"**

Actor 1: **"They say she used to play for the county."**

Actor 2: **"I can well believe it!"**

Actor 1: **"Well better run before I get thrashed again!"**

Actor 2: **"While you have a chance, hey?"**

Actor 1: **"Yes, exactly!"**

Actor 2: **"Good luck!"**

Actor 1: **"Thank you."**

Below is the previous dialogue explained line-by-line.

Actor 2: **"I say, Marianne is a bit of a whizz at tennis!"**

[this makes a compliment about somebody]

Actor 1: **"She is rather good, isn't she?"**

[this shows agreement with a question seeking your agreement]

Actor 2: **"She's more than good - she's beaten me three times this week!"**

[this shows an enthusiastic agreement with a self-deprecating comment]

Actor 1: **"They say she used to play for the county."**

[this offers new or supplementary information]

Actor 2: **"I can well believe it!"**

[this enthusiastically affirms understanding of information]

Actor 1: **"Well better run before I get thrashed again!"**

[this signals ending with a self-deprecating comment]

Actor 2: **"While you have a chance hey?"**

[this supports a reason]

Actor 1: **"Yes exactly!"**

[this is an enthusiastic agreement]

Actor 2: **"Good luck!"**

[this acknowledges the ending]

Actor 1: **"Thank you."**

[this confirms the ending]

Naturally, there are many more examples of set patterns for turn-taking in small talk. The two examples from the actors give you a feel for what the functions of the set patterns are.

Getting to grips with turn-taking

Naturally, small talk can have a wider variety of turn-taking. Turn-taking at speed during small talk can put people under pressure to respond quickly when they know it's their turn to say something. The pressure and the anticipation that they have to say something means that people divert their full attention to what they are about to say next, and by doing so, they divert their focus from listening to getting ready to speak. This is quite natural. The feeling of pressure and anticipation can be made worse when we are feeling nervous (for whatever reason) and this is a common cause of overlapping in turn-taking in small talk. What typically happens is the person hasn't waited until the other person has finished speaking - instead, they have probably unintentionally spoken over the top of what the other person is saying. Naturally, this gives the other person the impression that they are not being listened to and this can feel quite frustrating!

The more you can anticipate the set pattern of turn-taking, the more comfortable you are likely to feel with the speed of turn-taking. The speed at which people greet each other in small talk is very fast: "How are you? Fine, thanks. And you? Good, thanks." Speed is relative, so it might be slower or faster depending on your surroundings and the context of the greeting, but this example tends to be one of the fastest exchanges of turn-taking in small talk.

The film actors in the next example are playing characters from a contemporary setting. They are rehearsing their lines from a screenplay. The words in brackets and italics illustrate the function of the language being used in small talk.

Actor 1: **"What's happening?"**

Actor 2: **"Not a lot. You seen the match last night?"**

Actor 1: **"Couldn't be bothered. I knew who was going to win!"**

Actor 2: **"Right! It's been downhill all the way this season, hasn't it?"**

Actor 1: **"Yeah. Abysmal. You heading into town?"**

Actor 2: **"No. I'm waiting for Sheila to pick me up."**

Actor 1: **"Okay. So I'll see you next week then?"**

Actor 2: **"Yeah. Bye."**

Actor 1: **"See you."**

Below is the previous dialogue explained line-by-line.

Actor 1: **"What's happening?"**

[this is a general enquiry about surroundings]

Actor 2: **"Not a lot. You seen the match last night?"**

[this shows how to respond to an enquiry about surroundings and change the subject by asking a question]

Actor 1: **"Couldn't be bothered. I knew who was going to win!"**

[this is how to respond to the question and adds additional information with a level of certainty]

Actor 2: **"Right! It's been downhill all the way this season, hasn't it?"**

[this affirms understanding and agrees with a level of certainty and follows up with a question seeking further agreement]

Actor 1: "**Yeah. Abysmal. You heading into town?**"

[this is an agreement and supports the reason for agreement and then changes the subject by asking a question]

Actor 2: "**No. I'm waiting for Sheila to pick me up.**"

[this is how to respond to a question and then how to clarify the answer to the question]

Actor 1: "**Okay. So I'll see you next week then?**"

[this affirms understanding of information and follows up with a question regarding certainty about something]

Actor 2: "**Yeah. Bye.**"

[this confirms with certainty and then signals the end]

Actor 1: "**See you.**"

[this confirms the ending]

In this example, there is a wider variety of turn-taking in the small talk. The key to mastering successful small talk is not learning the phrases off by heart, but by knowing the patterns and functions of turn-taking. The two examples give you an impression of the type of functions used when turn-taking in small talk, but they are by no means all! Building up an understanding and experience in knowing which context uses specific functions in a set pattern is part of a person's flair in small talk.

Some of the pitfalls when listening in small talk

Listening is not something that comes naturally to humans. You just have to watch a child at play. The activity of 'playing' has the child's full attention, probably because the child is enjoying this activity.

A parent calls the child. It isn't immediately apparent to the child that their parent is calling them. Why is this? The most likely answer is that the child's maximum focus and attention has been directed toward the activity of playing. It's not easy for the child to keep an ear out for their parent's call *and* play fully. In other words, the child has decided not to listen out for their parent's call and instead has diverted their full attention to playing. This is probably why the parent has to call their child a number of times before the child realizes they are being called.

Children learn how to switch attention from one thing to another (from playing to responding to their parent's call) and they have to learn to do this at speed. The same could be said to happen when we are engaged in small talk. In small talk, the speed of turn-taking can also appear to go faster than in long conversations and discussions, when there is often more time to listen and reflect on what is being said and to think about what you want to say next.

Imagine this scenario. You are checking something important and you need to do it quickly. You have given this activity your full attention, and you are in the middle of the activity. You hear a person saying: *how are you?* You have experience to recognize that this question is directed to you. You respond in an instant, *fine thanks, and you?* You are still engaged in the checking activity. The person responds, *muggy, isn't it?* This response isn't what you were expecting to hear but because you are engrossed in your activity, you don't have time to call attention to it. You respond by saying: *yes, it is, isn't it?*

What could have happened here is that by putting your full focus and attention into the checking activity, you have missed the person's response, *fine thanks*. The fact that you didn't hear the person's response did not disrupt the flow of the small talk encounter. This shows the power of set patterns of turn-taking and using functions. Let's look at the use of functions in this small talk scenario.

Person: **"Muggy, isn't it?"**

[this is a statement about surroundings and a question seeking agreement]

You probably know that the set pattern of turn-taking requires the following function:

You: **"Yes, it is, isn't it?"**

[this shows agreement and follows up with a question seeking further agreement]

In this scenario, it is clear that even though your full attention was diverted to a different activity, it didn't matter too much. On the face of things, this scenario appears to be a successful display of small talk. Unfortunately, things don't always work out like this. That is why it is important for you to be aware of where your focus and attention are. This is because, if you have diverted your attention to a different activity, it is quite likely you might miss what someone says, and then it becomes obvious to the other person that you haven't been listening properly - probably because you haven't used the functions appropriately. This point is worth bearing in mind when engaging in small talk, as it can reveal how much you've been listening!

How can you make your small talk more effective?

Let's look at a possible scenario to see how your understanding of the use of functions can help you to make your small talk more effective. Imagine that a resident is helping an acquaintance to settle into their new surroundings. The surroundings and the people are familiar to the resident but not to the acquaintance.

Resident: **"How are you settling in?"**

Acquaintance: **"Good thanks. It's easier when someone knows the area well like you do."**

Resident: **"Some would say too well!"**

Acquaintance: "**When do people usually do their banking?**"

Resident: "**There are two banks on the high street and one in the shopping mall.**"

Acquaintance: "**So are there set times when people do their banking?**"

Resident: "**Yes, the banks are open from 8.30 to 4.**"

Acquaintance: "**I see. When do people prefer to go to the banks?**"

Resident: "**When they need to go I suppose. It's nice around here, isn't it?**"

Acquaintance: "**Yes, it's very nice.**"

Below is the previous dialogue explained line-by-line.

Resident: "**How are you settling in?**"
[this is a general enquiry about the person]

Acquaintance: **"Good thanks. It's easier when someone knows the area well like you do."**

[this responds positively to an enquiry and supports a reason for a positive response with a compliment]

Resident: **"Some would say too well!"**

[this makes a self-deprecating comment]

Acquaintance: **"When do people usually do their banking?"**

[this changes the subject by asking a question with a general enquiry about surroundings]

Resident: **"There are two banks on the high street and one in the shopping mall."**

[this shows how to respond to an enquiry about surroundings]

Acquaintance: **"So are there set times when people do their banking?"**

[this shows how to clarify the answer by asking a question]

Resident: **"Yes, the banks are open from 8.30 to 4."**

[this shows how to respond to the question and add additional information with a level of certainty]

Acquaintance: **"I see. When do people prefer to go to the banks?"**

[this confirms understanding and shows how to clarify the answer by asking a question]

Resident: **"When they need to go I suppose. It's nice around here, isn't it?"**

[this shows how to respond to an enquiry about surroundings and makes a statement about surroundings and follows up with a question seeking agreement]

Acquaintance: **"Yes, it's very nice."**

[this shows an enthusiastic agreement]

To develop your understanding of the functions and the context, see what you think about these questions:

Here are three questions for you:

1. What do you think was the main problem in this small talk situation?

2. How successful do you think the resident was at answering the acquaintance's questions?

3. How successful do you think the acquaintance was at responding to the resident's answers?

On the surface, the small talk encounter seems successful - both people took their turns to listen and to speak, and they also followed the set pattern of turn-taking by using the functions appropriately. However, an important function was missing in this small talk situation.

Let's look at the small talk scenario again. This time a new function has been used a number of times to clarify information by asking a question.

Resident: "How are you settling in?"

Acquaintance: "Good thanks. It's easier when someone knows the area well like you do."

Resident: "Some would say too well!"

Acquaintance: "When do people usually do their banking?"

Resident: "Sorry, did you say when or where?"

Acquaintance: "When."

Resident: "I see. Banks are open from 8.30 to 4"

Acquaintance: "Most people go banking first thing?"

Resident: "Actually they usually go at lunch times."

Acquaintance: "So are there set times for lunch around here?"

Resident: "Yes, people like to take their lunch around midday for about half an hour."

Acquaintance: "**I see. And that's when it gets busy in the banks?**"

Resident: "**Exactly - it can be bedlam in there!**"

Acquaintance: "**Best is to try to avoid that time like the plague then?**"

Resident: "**You've got it in one!**"

Below is the previous dialogue explained line-by-line.

Resident: "**How are you settling in?**"
[this is a general enquiry about the person]

Acquaintance: "**Good thanks. It's easier when someone knows the area well like you do.**"
[this responds positively to an enquiry and supports a reason for a positive response with a compliment]

Resident: **"Some would say too well!"**

[this *makes a self-deprecating comment*]

Acquaintance: **"When do people usually do their banking?"**

[*ask a question*]

Resident: **"Sorry, did you say when or where?"**

[*apologize and clarify information by asking a question*]

Acquaintance: **"When."**

[*respond to the question*]

Resident: **"I see. Banks are open from 8.30 to 4:00"**

[*confirm understanding and respond to the question with a level of certainty*]

Acquaintance: **"Most people go banking first thing?"**

[*clarify information by asking a question*]

Resident: **"Actually they usually go at lunch times."**

[offer new information to make something more precise]

Acquaintance: **"So there are set times for lunch around here?"**

[clarify information by asking a question]

Resident: **"Yes, people like to take their lunch around midday for about half an hour."**

[provide new information]

Acquaintance **"I see. And that's when it gets busy in the banks?"**

[clarify information by asking a question]

Resident: **"Exactly - it can be bedlam in there!"**

[offer enthusiastic agreement and support reason for positive agreement]

Acquaintance: **"Best is to try to avoid that time like the plague then?"**

[clarify information by asking a question]

Resident: **"You've got it in one!"**

[offer enthusiastic agreement]

Actually the acquaintance didn't get the information in one turn-taking move. It took five turn-taking moves for the resident to find out that banking at lunch times is the busiest time to go.

The acquaintance used the function of clarifying the information by asking a question to get the desired information. It seems like an obvious function to use but many people don't choose to do this because they don't want to pester the person with multiple questions! The acquaintance also used this function to check that the resident was listening, and in some respects, encouraged the resident to listen more attentively by using the function a number of times. Also, when the resident wasn't sure if the acquaintance has said 'when' or 'where' - the resident clarified this - showing the acquaintance friendly cooperative behavior.

How long should small talk last?

Small talk by connotation implies that it is small or short!

It is probably quite true that small talk is the first form of communication that occurs between people in a social setting, but not always, sometimes it can be the very last thing. Take, for example, a scenario where there has been an accident in a busy street with pedestrians, cyclists and cars. Passersby, including you, rush to the people involved in the accident. The police and ambulance are called. A police officer takes witness statements from you and other passersby, and then the police officer engages you and a passerby, whom you don't know, in a brief interlude of small talk. The small talk lasts just under a minute, but everyone took their turn to speak and everyone took their turn to listen.

In this accident scenario, the small talk lasted under a minute. This is probably because passersby were aware of the context and anticipated that the police officer may have other duties to attend to, and therefore, they don't want to detain the police officer longer than necessary. This seems reasonable. Also, the police officer might be adjusting a radio frequency, or writing something else down that comes to mind, so the actions of the police officer might indicate that the short talk interlude might be cut short or kept intentionally short.

In the accident scenario, your ability to read the social cues accurately and to understand the context by being aware of your surroundings will help you to decide how long the small talk should last.

Signalling an end to short talk

Signaling that you are coming to an end in short talk is not always easy because the context can be confusing or the social cues might be difficult to identify or read accurately. However, if you follow some of the advice in this book, you will feel more confident about how to do this without causing you (or others) any awkward or embarrassing moments.

Here is a checklist of questions you can use, when deciding when to signal an end to the small talk.

- What kind(s) of ending signals have you seen?

Ending signals like checking your watch, looking at a timetable or map, rolling up your sleeves, putting on your sunglasses or hat, or buttoning up your raincoat are all subtle social cues to alert someone that the small talk is about to come to a close.

- What kind(s) of ending signals have you heard?

Drawing in one's breath, sighing, pausing mid-sentence to check something that seems important, laughter, curt answers such as yes, no, maybe, phrases like "we'll see" and "you never know" are quite common ending signals.

These are not all of the ending signals that can be used and you may have your own personal favorites. However, it is vital that you pick up on ending signals or that you use them yourself. Signalling an ending is considered polite and it also minimizes embarrassing social situations by alerting people that the small talk is about to come to a close. This is a crucial element to small talk. Why not keep an ear and an eye out for ending signals the next time you are in your surroundings to see if you can identify these accurately? You may want to use them yourself in a small talk scenario of your own.

I've put together a special resources pack that I'll be adding to over time. These resources compliment the book. Download the action pack now and put some of the points raised here into action. The key to making changes in the way you talk with others is to apply small and measureable experiments and reflect on how they go. This resource pack will help you on your way to feeling comfortable in any social situation. Just click the link below:

Take action and get the free resources pack now!

Type this into your browser

http://smalltalkskills.com/book-resources

Chapter 6: Enhance Your Credibility In Small Talk Situations

Enhancing your credibility using the 3 C's of credibility

It may not be the first thing that springs to mind when thinking about your experiences in engaging in small talk, but presenting a credible impression of yourself to others is actually quite a useful way of looking at small talk. Your credibility, or at least other people's perceptions of your credibility, is a subconscious activity that is going on underneath the seemingly superficial air of small talk interludes. We may not always be aware of this.

But why is your credibility an important aspect of small talk? The reason is mainly because if you come across as being credible, you appear to others as being believable and trustworthy. The concept of creating a credible impression links to some of the reasons why people may choose to engage in small talk in the first place. For instance, if we want to present and support a positive self-image of ourselves as being polite, friendly, cooperative, and desirous of a harmonious and productive workplace or business relationship, we need to convince others of our credibility. In other words, you are trying to present yourself in the best light possible, but without going over the top! Also, some people may wish to influence what other people think of their position of power, authority and status by engaging in small talk in certain persuasive ways. They attempt to achieve this by enhancing their credibility in social situations. So how do people do this?

Aristotle was a Greek philosopher who thought long and hard about how a person can optimally achieve credibility in the eyes of others. His main ideas about credibility centered around the following four personal dimensions:

1. Trustworthiness: this is whether or not people perceive you as being trustworthy.

2. Similarity: this is other people's ability to identify with you or with your ability to identify with them.

3. Authority: this one can either be a formal authority (police controlling law and order) or an informal authority (parents supervising children).

4. Reputation: this is what other people know about you or have heard about you, and similarly, your impression of other people's reputations.

You may not feel all that concerned about your credibility. For some people, it is incredibly important perhaps because their roles in their jobs mean they need to create credibility so they are successful at work. It's worth having a think about whether or not credibility is important to you:

Here are three questions for you:

1. Is establishing a credible impression of yourself important in your job? Why?

2. Do you consider that credibility can be established via small talk? Why is that so?

3. How do you establish whether someone is credible or not?

Another way of looking at credibility is to think about how you assess someone's credibility, particularly someone you don't know very well or who is a stranger. When credibility has been studied in more recent times (1970's - 1990's), researchers found that credibility can be established by identifying specific aspects about one's character. Communication is also a crucial part of establishing one's credibility in other people's eyes - it often forms a large part of how we demonstrate our credibility to other people, and also how they use what we say or how we respond to what has been said, as a way to interpret and judge our credibility.

Here are the three C's of credibility:

1. **Competence**: Does the person seem to have a good or a bad reputation or a track record? Does the person hold a position of authority? If so, are they behaving responsibly?

2. **Character**: Does the person come across as being trustworthy and believable?

3. **Caring**: Is the person able to relate to you and to others around them even if there seem to be differences between people?

In an episode of the American sitcom *Friends*, Rachel and Phoebe challenge Ross's credibility. Ross tries to convince Rachel and Phoebe that he wants them to be safe. He claims that learning about self-defense is useless without the state of awareness of a Japanese concept called 'unagi'. He tries to demonstrate the importance of unagi when using self-defense by jumping out on them and trying to scare them.

Take a look for yourself. Type this into your browser: www.smalltalkskills.com/friends

We can use the 3 C's of credibility to establish if Ross appears credible when he says that he just wants Phoebe and Rachel to be safe. Let's look at this from Rachel and Phoebe's perspective.

Competence:

- Does Ross seem to have a reputation as an expert in 'unagi' and self-defense?

I think not. Phoebe and Rachel know that Ross isn't an expert in this area. They challenge his claim to expertise by telling him that unagi is a type of Japanese food.

- Does Ross behave responsibly?

I don't think so. Ross jumps out on Rachel and Phoebe and tries to scare them. However, his attempt to teach them a lesson in unagi seems to backfire on him. They seem more annoyed by Ross's behavior and decide to get their own back on Ross by jumping out from behind the curtains and surprising him.

Caring:

- Is Ross able to relate to Rachel and Phoebe?

It seems that Ross cares about Rachel and Phoebe because his intention is that he wants them to be safe. He goes to the effort of trying to teach them a lesson by jumping out on them in order to make his point about the importance of using unagi in self-defense. However, Phoebe and Rachel do not seem to respond well to Ross's behavior.

Character:

- Does Ross come across as being believable and trustworthy?

Not in this scenario. Phoebe in particular challenges Ross's credibility by telling him that unagi is actually a type of sushi made out of fresh water eel. Phoebe also tells Ross that he is a freak. Phoebe and Rachel clearly don't see Ross as being believable in this scenario because they decide to get their own back on him by jumping out on him when he is folding his clothes. Rachel then makes her point that unagi is in fact a 'salmon skin roll'.

How do you establish someone's credibility?

Usually speaking, people try their best to convey what they actually mean, but this isn't always the case. In unfamiliar surroundings and in the company of strangers, we have to use our social cues and social radar to quickly establish what is going on around us. The same is true when trying to figure out if what people are saying is actually what they mean, and also, whether what they mean accurately reflects their motives and intentions. In other words, whether we can trust and believe them, or not.

Are you a person who finds it hard to follow what people are saying, or who tends to take people at their word? If you receive mixed messages from a person, for example, when a person's body language contrasts sharply with what they are saying, this aspect of small talk can be particularly perplexing especially if you don't have a good grasp of the language or the culture.

Take again the scenario with the researcher who wishes to conduct surveys with members of the public. The researcher knows that in order to encourage a member of the public to do the survey, she will need to engage them in small talk first.

Your goal is to try to establish whether the researcher seems credible to you or not. If the researcher doesn't appear credible in your eyes, then the chances are you won't want to do the survey. Remember that the way you can establish a person's credibility is by thinking about the 3 C's: competence, character and caring.

Researcher: **"Are you interested in taking part in a public survey?"**

Passerby: **"Sorry, I'm actually running late and I'm in a rush, but when I'm on my way back I might have time then, okay?"**

Researcher: **"Yes sure."**

Half an hour later, you are walking along the same street where the researcher is standing.

Researcher: "Did you get to your appointment on time?"

Passerby: "I did. Thank you. So what is this survey about?"

Researcher: "It's about people's attitudes towards anti-social behavior in public places."

Passerby: "Well that is very apt, isn't it? Are many people doing the survey?"

Researcher: "There are spurts! Though there's a bit of a lull right now, as you can see."

Passerby: "Yes, people have gone home I guess. How long does the survey take?"

Researcher: "On average I would say between 8-10 minutes depending on what the person says. Some people have a lot to say, others don't, but saying something is important, isn't it?"

Passerby: "You're right. So what do I have to do?"

Researcher: "Okay. First I ask you some general questions about your day-to-day routine which involves public places and then I ask you some specific questions about your experiences of anti-social behavior. Does that sound okay?"

Passerby: "Yes, that part does. But what is the purpose of the survey?"

Researcher: "It's part of a larger government funded survey to understand the effects that anti-social behavior can have on members of the public and how they engage with others in public spaces. This research will eventually be available to many different types of people who need to know what members of the public currently think about anti-social behavior. Does that seem important to you?"

Passerby: "Yes, it does."

Researcher: "Good. Shall we begin the survey?"

Now let's have a look at the small talk situation again to understand how the member of public seeks to establish the researcher's credibility, and also how the researcher seeks to raise their credibility by using specific functions in small talk turn-taking.

Researcher: **"Are you interested in taking part in a public survey?"**

[making a general enquiry about the person demonstrates caring]

Passerby: **"Sorry, I'm actually running late and I'm in a rush, but when I'm on my way back I might have time then, okay?"**

[leave options open by not saying yes and not saying no]

Researcher: **"Yes sure."**

[enthusiastic agreement demonstrates character]

Half an hour later, you are walking along the same street where the researcher is standing.

Researcher: **"Did you get to your appointment on time?"**
[making a general enquiry about the person demonstrates caring]

Passerby: **"I did. Thank you. So what is this survey about?"**
[responding positively to an enquiry and changing the subject by asking a question demonstrates competence]

Researcher: **"It's about people's attitudes towards anti-social behavior in public places."**
[responding positively to an enquiry demonstrates competence]

Passerby: **"Well that is very apt, isn't it? Are many people doing the survey?"**
[enthusiastically affirming your understanding of information

and by making a general enquiry about your surroundings demonstrates caring]

Researcher: **"There are spurts! Though there's a bit of a lull right now, as you can see?"**
[enthusiastic agreement and a statement about your surroundings following with a question seeking your agreement demonstrates character]

Passerby: **"Yes, people have gone home I guess. How long does the survey take?"**
[agreeing with a level of certainty and supporting your reason for agreement and changing the subject by asking a question demonstrates competence]

Researcher: **"On average I would say between 8-10 minutes depending on what the person says."**
[responding to a question and adding additional information with a level of certainty demonstrates competence]

"Some people have a lot to say, others don't, but saying something is important, isn't it?"

[providing new information to make something more certain and asking a question seeking your agreement demonstrates caring]

Passerby: **"You're right."**

[this shows character]

"So what do I have to do?"

[making an agreement and changing the subject by asking a question demonstrates competence]

Researcher: **"Okay, first I ask you some general questions about your day-to-day routine which involves public places and then I ask you some specific questions about your experiences of anti-social behavior."**

[adding additional information with a level of certainty demonstrates competence]

"Does that sound okay?"

[clarifying information by asking a question demonstrates caring]

Passerby: **"Yes, that part does. But what is the purpose of the survey?"**

[this shows competence]

Researcher: **"It's part of a larger government funded survey to understand the effects that anti-social behavior can have on members of the public and how they engage with others in public spaces. This research will eventually be available to many different types of people who need to know what members of the public currently think about anti-social behavior."**

[adding additional pieces of information with a level of certainty shows competence]

"Does that seem important to you?"

[clarifying information by asking a question demonstrates caring]

Passerby: **"Yes, it does."**

[this shows character]

Researcher: **"Good. Shall we begin the survey?"**

[providing an enthusiastic response and asking a question seeking your agreement shows caring]

There are quite a lot of credibility aspects to explore in this extended small talk encounter, but the main points to identify are the following:

1. The member of public seeks to establish the researcher's credibility by asking four 'competency' functions, for example: [*change the subject by asking a question*]

2. The researcher seeks to establish credibility by answering with one 'character' function, and three 'competence' functions

3. The researcher seeks to establish credibility by asking six 'caring' functions

4. The member of public uses a caring function to establish whether the researcher is able to respond appropriately. In this example, the researcher responds by displaying something about their character in the hope that this enhances their level of credibility: [for example, providing an *enthusiastic agreement with a statement about surroundings and a question seeking your agreement*]

5. Specific small talk functions can be used to establish your perception of the level of someone's credibility, and likewise, using these functions appropriately can help you to establish your credibility in the eyes of others.

6. Try using these functions yourself to see what kind of insights you get into deciding whether a person is, from your point-of-view, credible or not.

How does 'perspective-taking' enhance your small talk skills?

The idea of 'perspective-taking' can sound like hocus-pocus.

Perspective-taking is a mindful activity in which we try to understand how a situation looks from another person's perspective. To explain why perspective-taking is important in small talk, it is necessary to explain the role of perspective-taking and how it helps humans to make certain types of decisions, such as, whether or not a person is likely to demonstrate cooperative behavior or competitive behavior.

Imagine a game of bluff. To win in a game of bluff, you have to:

"deceive your opponents by making them think, either that you are going to do something when you really have no intention of doing it, or that you have knowledge that you do not really have, or that you have something in your possession that you actually don't have."

In a game of bluff, it really does help if you have a poker face. This is when your face does not show what you are thinking or feeling. This is more difficult than it sounds.

There are various strategies which players can use to their advantage in a game of bluff. Perspective-taking can involve all or just some of the following:

1. Thinking about what other people think (about you or about others)

2. Thinking about other people's emotions (What are other people's visible or hidden emotions?)

3. Looking at other people's physical motives and intentions

4. Figuring out what other people's words actually mean (are they saying what they mean or not?)

5. Establishing what other people's belief systems and personal philosophies are

6. Finding out what other people's prior knowledge and experiences are

7. Guessing what other people's personalities are like.

To do well (or to win) in a game of bluff it is vital that you do these two things successfully:

1. Take your opponent's perspective;

2. Don't let your opponent know your perspective.

Why is the game of bluff so entertaining to many people around the world? Probably because it has something to do with the way humans are able to use perspective-taking to serve certain social purposes like, for example, getting on with people in a group or team, negotiating in business, resolving disagreements with family members and understanding other people's motives and intentions.

Now let's see how perspective-taking can be used when we engage in small talk.

As said before, the context in which small talk takes place and your particular surroundings are of vital importance when deciding whether or not to engage in small talk. Another way of looking at this is to decide whether you wish to cooperate in a small talk encounter. To more fully understand the idea about cooperative behavior in small talk, let's imagine a scenario that happened to me but could I suppose happen to anyone in a public place.

I'm sitting in a public park. I am alone. I'm reading something. Someone comes to sit near me. At first, I don't think about this because I am engrossed in my book. Then, suddenly, a thought comes to me, why has this person chosen to sit next to me? Then another thought comes to me, just a moment ago I was sitting here on my own, reading my book, and now this person has decided to sit next to me, and now I am wondering why this person has chosen to sit next to me, and since I have started to wonder why this is, I have started to have other thoughts about this person: What is this person like? What does this person want? Does the person look okay? Does the person intend to leave me alone or engage me in small talk? What if this person wants to harm me in some way?

Your train of thought could be quite different from mine. The point is up until the person decided to sit down near me, I wasn't thinking about the person, or what their motives were for sitting next to me.

Then I started to question my own behavior:

Have I done something to make the person want to sit next to me? Have I been sending out signals that I want company? Have I been behaving normally? Now, I really do have to monitor my own thoughts about the person to make sure that I don't come to the wrong conclusion. And now that since I am thinking these thoughts about the person and monitoring my own behavior, I am wondering if the person is having thoughts about me. What sorts of thoughts could these be? Is the person also monitoring their thoughts and behavior?

Sounds exhausting, doesn't it? In reality, these thoughts occur in seconds rather than minutes, and therefore, do not take up as much time as one would expect. Sometimes we dismiss these thoughts and sometimes we don't – again it all depends on the context.

Let's look more closely at the elements of perspective-taking which I illustrated in my scenario. This is my perspective-taking:

What the other person is thinking and *what the other person's physical motives and intentions are* and *what the person's emotions are.*

Do I find perspective-taking useful? Yes is my answer. I often use this technique to find out information about the following: the prior knowledge and experiences people have and what other people's personalities are like. In my view, using perspective-taking can contribute to successful small talk encounters, but I don't use it all the time!

I've put together a special resources pack that I'll be adding to over time. These resources compliment the book. Download the action pack now and put some of the points raised here into action. The key to making changes in the way you talk with others is to apply small and measureable experiments and reflect on how they go. This resource pack will help you on your way to feeling comfortable in any social situation. Just click the link below:

<u>Take action and get the free resources pack now!</u>

Type this into your browser

http://smalltalkskills.com/book-resources

Chapter 7: Social Cues To Give You Small Talk Clues

Are social cues really that helpful in small talk?

The social cues that present themselves to you are likely to vary from context to context - some social cues will only vary slightly and some might vary quite considerably. It all depends on where you are, what you are doing, who you are with and the people who are around you. The way we look at and perceive our surroundings is extremely important. It's like we have a pre-installed personal social monitoring system which helps us to process the information that we receive from our surroundings, and because we can monitor our social environments and systems, we are particularly adept at picking up social cues that tell us if we are going to be socially accepted or rejected.

Many people think that 'actions speak louder than words' and while this view may not be shared by everyone on this planet – the concept is a very important aspect of interacting with someone in small talk. Think back to the example with the parent, the child and the stranger on the bus. The first action that happened was the child dropped the toy; the second action was the stranger picked the toy up and handed it back to the child. No language had passed between them yet the actions of the stranger carried a lot of meaning especially for the parent. This action signified a friendly and cooperative gesture toward the parent (and also the child). This gesture was more than likely welcomed by the parent. Why? Because most parents would prefer that people display cooperative behavior toward them and their child rather than competitive or hostile behavior which would probably make a lot of people around them feel uncomfortable including themselves.

There is a lot of information on the Web about how to read social cues such as a person's body language, facial gestures and other nonverbal cues. Obviously, it can be fun to read this information to give you a general sense of what can happen when humans interact with each other, however, if we take some of this information too literally it can mean that we are using cues that we think are tried and tested to help us make good quality decisions even when we don't know if they work 100%. So, the advice here is to take the information on these websites with a healthy dose of skepticism.

One of the most well-known small talk scenarios is when a person wants to chat someone up because of a feeling of being attracted to this person. You have probably seen this scenario play out quite a number of times either in your day-to-day experiences or illustrated in poetry, literature, cinema and theatre plays. It's a scenario that receives a lot of attention from society mainly because it is fraught with potential awkward, embarrassing and possibly humiliating consequences. However, it also offers opportunities and prospects to develop friendships and intimate relationships that could last a long time. The concept of saving face in this context is extremely important and that is why your ability to offer opt ins and opt outs for yourself and the other person is crucial to successful small talk when attempting to chat up a person of the opposite sex (or same sex) because of a feeling of attraction. In fact, it is advisable to try to offer people opt in or opt out options during any small talk encounter particularly if you don't know the person. Offering a person options minimizes potentially awkward moments between strangers or acquaintances. There are numerous ways to offer options to the person you want to initiate small talk with. You need to find a way to offer options to the person that is sensitive to the context and appropriate to your surroundings. This point is very helpful to bear in mind when you are thinking about your small talk interactions with the opposite sex.

Imagine a scenario where you are attending a social gathering. There is a group of people and then there is an individual standing alone. You don't know anyone there.

Who would you approach first and why?

Imagine another scenario. You have locked yourself out of your car and your car keys are in the ignition. The driver's window is slightly wound down, but not enough for you to slip your arm down to reach your keys. You look around to see if anyone can help you. You see two groups of people, a group of teenagers and a group of pensioners.

Who would you ask to help you? Would you wait for somebody else to come by?

It seems that to help us make choices during these scenarios, we have an inbuilt social radar that helps us to find a person or group of people who we think are going to accept our social advances, and therefore, be more likely to engage in small talk with us in a polite, friendly and cooperative manner. It is also conceivable that our inbuilt social radar helps us to locate men or women and people of different ages because certain contexts will influence who we choose to engage with in small talk. We have to trust that our social radar works!

Who should make the first move in small talk: men or women?

A popular assumption is that women take more opportunities to engage in small talk than men because they like to talk more. If this were true, then more women than men would make the first move to engage in small talk. Is the first move made only because a woman wants to talk to someone? However, a contradictory and widely held assumption is that a man is more likely to make the first move with a woman in small talk because he wants to attract her attention. Is the first move made by a man only because he wants to get her attention? Does making the first move (taking the first turn) signify something different if a man does it or if a woman does it? The answer to these questions will depend very much on the context and can't assume anything based solely on a person's gender, as assumptions can lead to misunderstandings between people.

Imagine these scenarios:

A woman takes the first turn (the first move) to engage people, who happen to be male, in small talk. Why would this be?

A man approaches a woman in a busy precinct. He takes the first turn (the first move) to engage her in small talk. Is he trying to chat her up?

Accurately reading the context is vital to your understanding of what is going on between people, and this includes what is going on with you! The woman in the park may have lost her dog and the man chases after the woman because she left her coat behind in a café. We can't make assumptions based solely on what we think we see. We should wait and try to read the social cues and the context before making up our minds.

Obviously, it is also folly to surmise that the person who takes the first turn in small talk is always going to be a woman! It is also folly to surmise that when a man takes the first turn with a woman it is only because he is attracted to her.

What is important is to try to identify and understand the social cues you are using to make judgments about what is going on around you and also to read what might be going on with the other speaker(s) in small talk situations.

How do you deal with those awkward moments?

Awkward small talk moments do happen from time to time and it can happen when you least expect it. This is probably why some people find small talk quite challenging - it can be quite embarrassing at times. One of the most common problems with small talk is when both speakers start to say something at the same time. They appear to speak over the top of each other. This doesn't seem too much of a problem if it happens once or twice. To resolve this, usually one of the speakers invites the other one to say something first. It's like restarting a stopwatch. However, things can get a little awkward if the overlapping happens again. It's not really anyone's fault - it just happens from time to time. So, what can you do if this happens to you?

Try to think about why you want to say something first:

1. Is it because you are in a rush?

2. Is it because your mind is on something else that is bothering you?

3. Is it because you really want to please or impress someone?

4. Is it because you don't actually feel comfortable in that person's company?

5. Is there something about your surroundings that is affecting your sense of small talk timing?

Try to pinpoint what it is that might be throwing you off balance. If you can't identify anything for yourself, then try to identify if there is something going on with the person with whom you are speaking. You will need to try to pick up on the social cues around you to help you identify what might be causing the other person to overlap in turn-taking.

If you feel you need to do something about the overlapping in your turn-taking, you could try these tips:

1. Slow things down by showing the other speaker that you are observing your surroundings. This means that you can slightly avert your eyes away from the speaker or slightly turn your head so that you have a different view. This small movement can slow down the tempo just enough for each person to reset or to adjust their 'turn-taking rhythm'.

2. Add in a little laugh! Don't laugh at the person but use a little laugh to lighten the awkward moment. If you don't feel comfortable laughing, then smile instead. When you add a little laugh (or smile), you are acknowledging that the turn-taking isn't working out, and that you are going to attempt to get the turn-taking back on track. Also, by not speaking, you are signaling to the other person that speaking isn't the most important aspect at that very moment and that you are aware that something else might help to reset the 'turn-taking clock'.

3. Try not to say, "I'm sorry" or "Sorry, you go first" because this will act as prompt for another turn-taking

pattern which requires the other speaker to say, "No, sorry, you go first" or "Please you first" or something to that effect. This can cause an even greater amount of embarrassment and inevitably makes the reason to continue engaging in small talk less appealing to you (and the other speaker).

4. Instead of saying "I'm sorry, you go first" - use a friendly hand gesture to signal or to invite the other person to say something first. The hand gesture should be open, so for example, your palm should be facing upwards and you should outstretch your palm very slightly but just enough for the speaker to see it in their peripheral vision. The hand gesture should be inviting, subtle and expressive of the desire for continued communication.

Removing yourself from uncomfortable small talk situations

Unfortunately, there may well be times when you may feel that the small talk situation is not going well and that you are feeling negative vibes during the small talk encounter. The range of negative vibes might be causing you to feel a range of emotions from confused, uneasy, upset, awkward, uncomfortable, flummoxed, hesitant, embarrassed and even humiliated.

So what can you do when you experience any one or more of these emotions?

Obviously, if you are feeling any of these emotions then you must pay attention to them, and take them seriously, because it might be that your intuition and social radar might be sending you messages which provide you with vital clues to help you to work out what is going on and what course of action you should take.

Firstly, you should try to get a good understanding of what you think is happening. If you have tried to read the situation, and you are still not sure what is happening, then you need to make a couple of decisions, and this comes back to a basic human reaction to a perceived threat. The threat could be either a physical or verbal threat or both. It's known as flight-or-fight. In other words, should you stay or should you go? Only you can make this decision, and you will need to use your intuition as well as your social radar to sense how dangerous the threat is to your well-being. There is no easy way to explain how this actually feels or works in practice but your appropriate response to the situation is crucial.

How should I remove myself from a negative small talk encounter?

The best way to do this is to use these strategies to match the level of negativity or threat that you are experiencing:

1. Use one-word answers, such as yes or no. Do not use functions in the set patterns of turn-taking, as this is likely to encourage the person to continue engaging you in small talk.

2. Shift your gaze distinctly away from the person or people. Avoid reconnecting with the person/people by averting your gaze away even if you are asked a question. This is quite a strong signal to the other person that something is wrong and that you do not wish to continue engaging in small talk.

3. If it is appropriate, try to establish a connection with another person who isn't a threat to you. Try to avoid facial gestures, such as a smile, a look, a scowl because these could easily be misinterpreted by others around you and cause misunderstandings. Try to sit or

stand near friendly looking people instead which is a clear sign that you are feeling negatively toward the other person or people you were engaged in small talk with, and that you are signaling to the friendly looking people that you may need their help or protection.

4. If this isn't appropriate, try to identify things around you that could be of use to you. For example, is there a door, such as, a sign to a toilet/bathroom/WC? Or a shop you could pop into? Is there a taxi you could hail quickly?

5. Work out your escape plan. Make as simple a plan as possible and stick to it. Do not allow anyone to make you deviate from your escape plan. Your sense of self-preservation has most likely kicked in for a good reason, and you need to take it very seriously.

I've put together a special resources pack that I'll be adding to over time. These resources compliment the book. Download the action pack now and put some of the points raised here into action. The key to making changes in the way you talk with others is to apply small and measureable experiments and reflect on how they go. This resource pack will help you on your way to feeling comfortable in any social situation. Just click the link below:

<u>Take action and get the free resources pack now!</u>

Type this into your browser

http://smalltalkskills.com/book-resources

Chapter 8: Tips On Getting The Most From Your Small Talk Encounters

Thinking outside the small talk box

A lot of people get quite apprehensive about engaging in small talk when they have to do it in a foreign language or in a cultural place that is unfamiliar to them. This is understandable. However, it does help to try to concentrate on the positives rather than the negative aspects. One of the most positive aspects about small talk is that the universal features of small talk typically involve quite a lot of social cues. Social cues can be a mixture of words and actions, but similarly, it can be a selection of words or actions. A well-known example of this is a social scenario when one person wants to enter through a door and the other person wants to exit via the same door. This scenario involves two strangers entering and exiting a shop via the same shop door.

Imagine how the following scenario plays out between the two strangers.

The exiting person sees the other person first and understands that the person wants to enter, so the exiting person steps aside slightly and gestures for the person to enter. The person enters the door by pushing the door open, while the exiting person holds the door open for the person until they have fully entered the shop. The exiting person then leaves the shop.

In this scenario, not a word passed between the two people but it didn't seem to matter. The people involved could have used language if they had wanted to, but possibly in this context both people decided that it actually wasn't necessary. So, what we can say is that sometimes in small talk language is not always necessary. This point is worth linking to the idea mentioned previously about social cues and how we use actions to interpret what is going on around us.

The questions you should be asking yourself are:

1. Does the action display friendly and cooperative behavior toward me (or others)?

2. How have I interpreted other people's actions?

By trying to answer these questions, you should feel more at ease with dealing with new or unfamiliar small talk situations.

Practical strategies to try at home and in social situations

It might be that you are quite new to small talk and that you are currently building up your experiences of how small talk works and also how it doesn't work. Sharing these experiences with people like your friends, family members and close colleagues can actually prove quite illuminating. Also, you can encourage them to tell you about their small talk experiences - both good and bad! It might also help you to ask the person whose experience it was to tell you what aspects they think made the small talk successful or unsuccessful. You can imagine some anecdotes might be quite funny too!

One of the hardest things to do in small talk is to understand other people's belief systems and personal life philosophies. Most people would advise to act cautiously when trying to do this and many might suggest that for a typical small talk encounter with a stranger there is no need to establish this. However, establishing these aspects in other people can be really useful. This can be extremely important in certain contexts and small talk situations, for instance, when you start a new job and you need to get to know your new coworkers, working with new clients, making new acquaintances, and presenting information to a new audience. This is particularly useful when you are in a new social setting, like going to university for the first time, starting a new job, joining a sports club, going to a gym or making friends in a new community group. It can be important in certain contexts to establish what belief systems people have because, to a certain extent, belief systems and personal philosophies will influence the way that people engage with you in small talk and vice versa. Your own belief system and personal philosophies might influence how you approach engaging others in small talk.

Let's revisit the scenario when I was sitting in a public park and a stranger sat near me even though there was plenty of space for the person to sit in other parts of the park.

As you may recall, the first question I asked myself was: why has this person chosen to sit next to me? To help me answer this question, I engaged in perspective-taking. The questions I asked sought to establish what *my* perspective was of the person, such as:

1. What is the person like?
2. Does the person look okay?

The second question I asked myself was actually the same question, but this time I tried to answer it from the person's perspective. The questions I used to help me establish this actually focused on what the person's perspective *of me* might be, such as:

1. What does this person want? (What do I think they want from me?)
2. Does the person intend to leave me alone or engage me in small talk? (What do I think their motives are?)
3. What if this person wants to harm me in some way? (Why would the person want to cause me harm?)

These are only examples of the types of questions you might ask in this scenario. The point is to show how quickly perspective-taking shifts from establishing what your perspective is to establishing what the other person's perspective might be. It's important to highlight the word 'might' because we can never 100% know the mind of others, just as other people can never 100% know our minds.

Let's imagine how this scenario might play out between the person reading a book in the public park (the 'reader') and the person who sits next to the reader (the 'sitter'). The reader is engrossed in the book. The sitter isn't doing anything in particular apart from sitting down.

Sitter: **"Hot weather today!"**

Reader: **"Yes."**

Sitter: "What are you reading?"

Reader: "A book. It's very good."

Sitter: "Are you nearly coming to the end?"

Reader: "No, I don't think so."

Sitter: "I like to read."

Reader: "Me too."

Sitter: "What sort of things do you like to read?"

Reader: "Anything really."

Sitter: "Would you like to read something I have written?"

Reader: "I can only read one thing at a time I'm afraid."

Sitter: "Oh that's okay. You can take it away to read, if you like?"

Reader: "Well, yes okay. What is it?"

Sitter: "It's a pamphlet about seeking guidance."

Reader: "Okay, well thanks."

Sitter: "You are welcome. This is my last one, but seeing you looked lonely I thought it might be a nice thing to do."

Reader: "Oh, okay well thank you."

Sitter: "Anytime. My name is Sam by the way."

Reader: "I'm Alex. I'm new here."

Sitter: "I thought as much!"

Reader: "Oh, why is that?"

Sitter: "Because none of the locals sit under this tree. It's full of bees, haven't you noticed?"

Reader: "So it is! Thank you for telling me."

Sitter: "That's okay. I have got to go now but maybe see you around sometime?"

Reader: *"Sure, but not under this tree right?"*

Sitter: **"Right. We tend to sit over there where it's cool and breezy."**

Reader: **"Great, thanks for the tip!"**

Sitter: **"Okay, well see you."**

Reader: **"See you."**

Sitter: **"Oh Alex, I didn't really write that pamphlet, but you can use it to swat the bees if they come near you."**

Reader: **"Okay, thanks*!*"**

Below is the previous dialogue explained line-by-line.

Sitter: **"Hot weather today!"**

Reader: **"Yes."**
[What I'm thinking is what is the person like?]

Sitter: **"What are you reading?"**

Reader: **"A book. It's very good."**

[What I'm thinking is does the person look okay?]

Sitter: **"Are you nearly coming to the end?"**

Reader: **"No, I don't think so."**

[What I'm thinking is What does this person want?]

Sitter: **"I like to read."**

Reader: **"Me too."**

[What I'm thinking is does this person intend to leave me alone or engage me in small talk?]

Sitter: **"What sort of things do you like to read?"**

Reader: **"Anything really."**

[What I'm thinking is why do they want to engage with me in small talk?]

Sitter: **"Would you like to read something I have written?"**

Reader: **"I can only read one thing at a time I'm afraid."**
[What I'm thinking is what motives does this person have?]

Sitter: **"Oh that's okay. You can take it away to read, if you like?"**

Reader: **"Well, yes okay. What is it?"**
[What I'm thinking is why does this person want to give me this?]

Sitter: **"It's a pamphlet about seeking guidance."**

Reader: **"Okay, well thanks."**
[What I'm thinking is what religion is this person trying to impose on me?]

Sitter: "You are welcome. This is my last one, but seeing you looked lonely I thought it might be a nice thing to do."

Reader: "Oh, okay well thank you."
[What I'm thinking is do I really look that lonely?]

Sitter: "Anytime. My name is Sam by the way."

Reader: "I'm Alex. I'm new here."
[What I'm thinking is why am I telling this person this?]

Sitter: "I thought as much!"

Reader: "Oh, why is that?"
[What I'm thinking is this person has got my attention]

Sitter: "Because none of the locals sit under this tree. It's full of bees, haven't you noticed?"

Reader: **"So it is! Thank you for telling me."**

{What I'm thinking is this person is considerate}

Sitter: **"That's okay. I have got to go now but maybe see you around sometime?"**

Reader: **"Sure, but not under this tree right?"**

[What I'm thinking is what have I got to lose by being friendly?]

Sitter: **"Right. We tend to sit over there where it's cool and breezy."**

Reader: **"Great, thanks for the tip!"**

[What I'm thinking is this person is really helpful]

Sitter: **"Okay, we'll see you."**

Reader: **"See you."**

Sitter: **"Oh Alex, I didn't really write that pamphlet, but you can use it to swat the bees if they come near you."**

Reader: **"Okay, thanks!"**

[What I'm thinking is this person lied and then told me the truth, but what motives did this person have to do so?]

This scenario shows a range of perspective-taking from the reader's point of view. The reader's perspective alternates from establishing a perspective about the sitter, to establishing what the sitter's perspective might be, back to establishing a different perspective about the sitter and trying to understand what the sitter's motives might be. The reader also tests an assumption about the sitter's belief system: for instance {*what religion is this person trying to impose on me?*} By engaging in continued small talk with the sitter, the reader is able to establish some information about the sitter's personal philosophy:

For instance [*this person lied and then told me the truth but what motives did this person have to do so?*]

You too can try using specific functions to practice perspective-taking which can form part of your strategy to establish other people's belief systems and personal philosophies. Let's look at the sorts of perspective-taking questions that the sitter (Sam) may have asked when trying to decide whether or not to approach the reader (Alex) and engage in a small talk situation:

What am I thinking about the person?

1. Does the person look okay?

2. What is the person like?

3. What might this person want from me?

What are my physical motives and intentions?

1. What social cues have I picked up on to decide whether to sit down next to this person?

2. What motives do I have to sit near this person?

What is the other person thinking?

1. What does this person need?

2. Does this person look like they want to be left alone or could they be interested in engaging with me in small talk?\

What are the person's emotions?

1. Why would this person open up to me?

Things worth remembering about small talk

The most important thing to remember about small talk is that even though it might seem superficial, self-serving, boring and generally speaking not worth the effort, there can be times when it is beneficial for you to engage others in small talk and for you to be open to the possibility of engaging in small talk with others.

Sometimes the smallest moments in our lives are the times when we realize how much we interact in other people's worlds as well they do in our own, and how important these interactions can be - not just for ourselves but for others too. It's times like these when you:

1. See a child's beaming smile when you pick up their favorite toy and hand it back

2. Share your amusement with another person when everyone else is looking down at their mobile phones and you are the only two people looking up

3. Share an appreciation of the fine weather you've been having recently

4. Gently acknowledge someone's humility when you compliment them on something they have done well

5. Help each other feel calmer after witnessing an accident

6. Don't ignore someone when they are doing their job and not being ignored when you are doing your job

7. Offer to help someone when they look lost

8. Pass the time pleasantly with someone while waiting to be picked up from work

9. Invite someone to enter through a door first and then hold the door open

10. Get to know someone with whom you develop a friendship

All of these moments are examples of small talk! Some examples involve talking and some don't. But they do require you to be concentrating or focusing, so that you get the most benefit out of these small yet sometimes quite pleasurable moments.

Even if you don't speak the language, or you don't consider that you communicate fluently; it doesn't matter - the universal nature of small talk (without the talking) means that it typically works wherever you go!

Have fun with your small talk and try to seek out small pleasures of being in the moment with people you may never see again, or with whom you might develop meaningful relationships. Whichever it turns out to be - these memories make your life, **your** life! So don't hold back from small talk – it could mean the start of something beautiful.

I've put together a special resources pack that I'll be adding to over time. These resources compliment the book. Download the action pack now and put some of the points raised here into action. The key to making changes in the way you talk with others is to apply small and measureable experiments and reflect on how they go. This resource pack will help you on your way to feeling comfortable in any social situation. Just click the link below:

<u>Take action and get the free resources pack now!</u>

Type this link into your browser:

http://smalltalkskills.com/book-resources

Final Words

I hope that you have enjoyed learning about small talk and enjoy chatting to other people with your enhanced small talk skills.

Remember that it takes time to master any skill whether you are starting out or making improvements to your communication skills.

Whenever you are struggling with the next small talk words to try, remember to use this reference guide and reflect on how well you have progressed. I hope you build great new relationships with small talk and enjoy getting out there and meeting new people.

Appendix

Here is a handy list of functions for you to use in your small talk encounters. For each function, I have provided an example to remind you of what you could say.

Functions to **make** the **first move** in turn-taking:

1. *[general enquiry about the person]* "**Everything okay?**"
2. *[general enquiry about surroundings]* "**Is it normal for it to be so muggy at this time of the year?**"
3. *[statement about surroundings]* "**It's really cold and windy today.**"
4. *[question seeking other person's agreement]* "**It's not usually closed now, is it?**"

Functions to **respond** to the **first move** in turn-taking:

1. *[respond positively to enquiry]* "**Really great, thanks.**"
2. *[respond to enquiry about surroundings]* "**The best coffee shop is a little way down the street**"
3. *[support reason for positive response/agreement]* "**And I can see why she got a round of applause!**"
4. *[offer new information expressing uncertainty]* "**It could change tomorrow but then again it might not.**"

Functions to convey **agreement**:

1. *[agreement]* **"No worries."**
2. *[enthusiastic agreement]* **"Absolutely!"**
3. *[confirm understanding]* **"I see."**
4. *[enthusiastically affirm understanding of information]* **"Yes, it could just be the best time to visit."**

Functions to convey **certainty**:
1. *[offer new information to make something more certain]* **"So it might be a busy period then?"**
2. *[affirm understanding of information]* **"I get it."**
3. *[agree with level of certainty]* **"You're most likely right."**

Functions to **clarify information**:

1. *[change the subject by asking a question]* **"Is it your first visit to Italy?"**
2. *[clarify the question]* **"So what you're asking me is if it's open today?"**
3. *[clarify information by asking a question]* **"What happens around here in the evenings then?"**

Functions to convey **uncertainty**:

1. *[statement of uncertainty]* **"Well I'm not sure if that has happened before."**

2. *[offer new information expressing uncertainty]* **"Well that could be true."**

Functions to **compliment** someone and to respond to a compliment:

1. *[compliment somebody]* **"So you're looking really well."**

2. *[make a self-deprecating comment]* **"Well I'm trying my best to look presentable."**

Functions to signal small talk is **ending**:

1. *[signals to end]* **"Time flies when you're having fun!"**

2. *[confirms ending]* **"And even faster when you're not looking!"**

Glossary

Chit-chat: 'informal conversation about matters that are not important': (Cambridge online dictionary)

Example: **"What did you talk about?" "Oh, just chit-chat."**

Conversation: 'talk between two or more people in which thoughts, feelings, and ideas are expressed, questions are asked and answered, or news and information is exchanged'. (Cambridge online dictionary)

Example: **"It was a really interesting conversation, one that will stay with me for the rest of my life."**

Discussion: 'the activity in which people talk about something and tell each other their ideas or opinions': (Cambridge online dictionary)

Example: **"Management are holding or having discussions with employee representatives about possible redundancies."**

Pleasantry or pleasantries: 'a polite and often slightly humorous remark, usually made to help other people feel relaxed': (Cambridge online dictionary)

Example: **"After exchanging pleasantries, the delegation revealed the purpose of their visit."**

Your Bonus Gift

I want to thank you for supporting my work

so I've put together this bonus free gift for you.

I'll be adding more useful learning resources in time

so be sure to check this out

Download the gift
by going to: http://smalltalkskills.com/book-resources

Urgent Plea!

Thank you again for downloading my book!

I really appreciate all of your feedback and I love hearing about what you have to share.

I need your input to make the next version of this book better.

I'm always learning from people like you

so please leave me a helpful REVIEW on Amazon by turning the page or visiting
http://www.amazon.com/Small-Talk-Effortlessly-Conversations-Confidence-ebook/dp/B00MBXVXL4/.

Thanks so much!!

Betty Bohm

Printed in Great Britain
by Amazon.co.uk, Ltd.,
Marston Gate.